Learn to Play

LEVEL 1
BLUES GUITAR

Method by John McCarthy

Written and Adapted by Steve Gorenberg

Supervising Editor: Joe Palombo
Layout, Graphics and Design: Steve Gorenberg
Photography: Joe Palombo, Scott Sawala
Audio Engineer: Joe Cuzino

Copy Editors and Proofreaders:
Alex Palombo, Cathy McCarthy, Irene Villaverde

Cover Art Direction and Design:
Sarah Dekin and Jennifer Pienkoski

ISBN: 0-9764347-5-X

Produced by The Rock House Method®

Table of Contents

John McCarthy
author of
The Rock House Method

John is a virtuoso guitarist who has worked with some of the industry's most legendary musicians. He has the ability to break down, teach and communicate music in a manner that motivates and inspires others to achieve their dreams of playing an instrument.

John is the creator of **The Rock House Method**®, the world's leading musical instruction method. Over his 20 year career, he has produced and/or appeared in more than 100 instructional products. Millions of people around the world have learned to play music using John's easy to follow, accelerated program.

As a guitarist and songwriter, John blends together a unique style of Rock, Metal, Funk and Blues in a collage of melodic compositions, jam-packed with masterful guitar techniques. His sound has been described as a combination of vintage guitar rock with a progressive, gritty edge that is perfectly suited for today's audiences.

Throughout his career, John has recorded and performed with renowned musicians like Doug Wimbish, Grammy winner Leo Nocentelli, Rock & Roll Hall of Famer Bernie Worrell, David Ellefson, Will Calhoun, Jordan Giangreco and Alex Bach. He has also shared the stage with Blue Oyster Cult, Kansas, Al Dimeola and Dee Snyder.

For more information on John, his music and his instructional products, visit www.rockhousemethod.com.

CREATING MUSICIANS
ONE LESSON AT A TIME

Introduction

Welcome to *The Rock House Method*® system of learning. You are joining millions of aspiring musicians around the world who use our easy-to-understand methods for learning to play music.

Unlike conventional learning programs, *The Rock House Method*® is a four-part teaching system that employs DVD, CD and 24/7 online lesson support along with this book to give you a variety of sources to assure a complete learning experience. Each product can be used individually or together. The DVD that comes with this book matches the curriculum exactly, providing you with a live instructor for visual reference. You can pause, rewind, or fast forward any lesson. In addition, the DVD contains some valuable extras like sections on changing your strings, guitar care, and an interactive chord library. The CD that we've included lets you take your lessons with you anywhere you go.

How to use the lesson support site

Every Rock House product offers FREE membership to our interactive Lesson Support site. Use the member number included with your book to register. You will find it on the sleeve that contains your DVD and CD. Go to www.hob.com, click the icon on their home page and you will be taken to The Rock House Method Lesson Support site. Once registered, you will use this fully interactive site along with your product to enhance your learning experience, expand your knowledge, link with instructors, and connect with a community of people around the world who are learning to play music using *The Rock House Method*®. There are sections that directly correspond to this product within the *Additional Information* and *Backing Tracks* sections. There are also a variety of other tools you can utilize such as *Ask The Teacher*, *Quizzes*, *Reference Material*, *Definitions*, *Forums*, *Live Chats*, *Guitar Professor* and much more.

Icon Key

Throughout this book, you'll periodically notice the following icons. They indicate when there are additional learning tools available on our support website for the section you're working on. When you see an icon in the book, visit the member section of www.rockhousemethod.com for musical backing tracks, additional information and learning utilities.

Backing Track

Many of the exercises in this book are intended to be played along with bass and drum rhythm tracks. This icon indicates that there is a backing track available on our support site for that particular lesson. You can download these tracks and create a CD to practice with.

Additional Information

The question mark icon indicates there is more information for that section available on the website. It can be theory, more playing examples, or tips.

Metronome

Metronome icons are placed next to the examples that we recommend you practice using a metronome. You can download a free, adjustable metronome from the support site.

Tablature

This icon indicates that there is additional guitar tablature available on the website that corresponds to the lesson. There is also an extensive database of tab music online that is updated regularly.

Tuner

Also found on the website is free tuner software which you can download to help you tune your instrument.

CHAPTER 1

Essential Blues Tools

Solid Body Electric Guitar

The solid body electric is the standard electric guitar that's great for distortion sounds and lead playing. Pickups mounted on the guitar's body send the sound to an amplifier. If there are two (or more) pickups, a pickup selector switch (*toggle switch*) is used to select one or blend them together. Pickups located near the bridge (*bridge pickups*) tend to have a brighter sound, making them better suited for lead playing. Pickups closer to the neck (*neck pickups*) have a warmer sound, making them a good choice for rhythm playing. A humbucker pickup is a popular double coil pickup designed to cancel electronic hum.

Acoustic Guitar

An acoustic guitar is an ideal choice for intimate performances, classic blues, fingerpicking, country, or bluegrass. The sound is projected out from the body of the guitar through the sound hole, making an amplifier unnecessary. An acoustic/electric is a type of acoustic guitar with built in pickups, allowing it to be amplified through an amp or PA system.

Hollow Body Electric Guitar

A hollow body electric guitar is a hybrid of the regular acoustic and electric guitars. It has F-holes on the front of the body, allowing the sound to resonate. These guitars are the choice of many classic blues and slide guitarists.

Picks

There are many different types of picks in different thicknesses. A heavy pick may offer you more control for lead playing, but medium and light picks have a flexibility that's good for rhythm playing.

Strings

Strings are available in different gauges. Heavier gauge strings produce a thicker, fuller sound; lighter gauges are thinner, easier to bend, and great for soloing.

Tuning

Each of the six strings on a guitar is tuned to and named after a different note (*pitch*). The thinnest or 1st string is referred to as the highest string because it is the *highest sounding* note. The thickest or 6th string is referred to as the lowest string because it is the *lowest sounding* note. Memorize the names of the open strings. These notes form the basis for finding any other notes on the guitar.

Names of the Open Strings

6th string	5th string	4th string	3rd string	2nd string	1st string
E	A	D	G	B	E

6th string (thickest)
lowest sounding string

1st string (thinnest)
highest sounding string

Tune your guitar using the machine heads on the headstock. Turn the machine heads a little bit at a time while plucking the string and listening to the change in pitch. Tighten the string to raise the pitch. Loosen the string to lower the pitch. Be careful not to accidentally break a string by tightening it too much or too quickly.

The easiest way to tune a guitar is to use an electronic tuner. There are many different kinds available that are fairly inexpensive. You can also download the free online tuner from www.rockhousemethod.com.

Reading a Chord Chart

A chord chart (*chord diagram*) is a graphic representation of part of the fretboard (as if you stood the guitar up from floor to ceiling and looked directly at the front of the neck). The vertical lines represent the strings; the horizontal lines represent the frets.

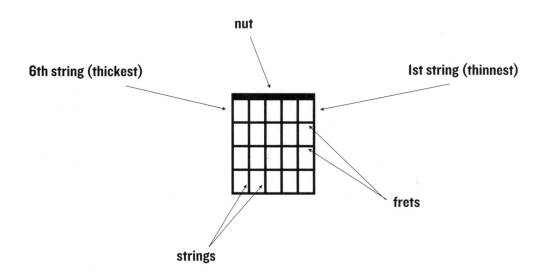

Chord diagrams show which notes to play and which strings they are played on. The solid black dots within the graph represent fretted notes and show you where your fingers should go. Each of these dots will have a number directly below it, underneath the diagram. These numbers indicate which left hand finger to fret the note with (1 = index, 2 = middle, 3 = ring, 4 = pinky). The 0s at the bottom of the diagram show which strings are played open (strummed with no left hand fingers touching them).

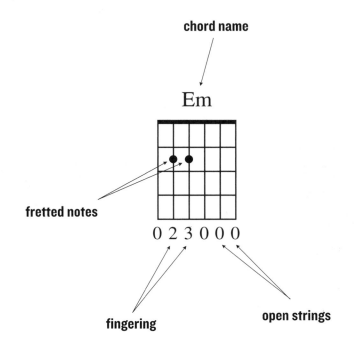

9

Open Blues Chords

Open Major Chords

The following open major chords are the most commonly used in rock and blues progressions. These three chords, **A**, **D**, and **E**, represent the **I - IV - V** (*one - four - five*) chords in the key of A major. The roman numerals refer to the steps of the scale, relative to what key the music is in. The A chord is the **I** chord (also called the *tonic*). The D chord is the **IV** chord (also called the *subdominant*) because in the key of A, D is the fourth step of the scale. Finally, the **V** chord (or *dominant*) is the E chord, because E is the fifth step of the scale in the key of A. To find the I - IV - V chords in any key, build chords on the 1st, 4th and 5th degrees of the scale.

The I - IV - V chord progression is the foundation that all rock and blues was built on and has evolved from. There are many variations, but songs such as "Johnny B. Goode," "You Really Got Me," "Rock and Roll," "I Love Rock and Roll" and "Sympathy for the Devil" are all based on the I - IV - V.

In the **A** chord diagram, the slur going across the notes means you should *barre* (bar) those notes. A barre is executed by placing one finger flat across more than one string. Pick each note of the chord individually to make sure you're applying enough pressure with your finger. Notice that the 6th and 1st strings each have an "x" below them on the diagram, indicating these strings are not played (either muted or not strummed). For each chord, the first photo shows what the chord looks like from the front. The second photo is from the player's perspective.

A

x 0 1 1 1 x

D

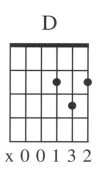

x 0 0 1 3 2

E

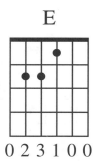

0 2 3 1 0 0

Open Minor Chords

Here are the I - IV - V chords in the key of A minor: **Am**, **Dm** and **Em**. Minor chords have a sad or melancholy sound, whereas the major chords have a bright or happy sound.

Am

x 0 2 3 1 0

Dm

x 0 0 2 3 1

Em

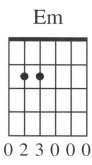

0 2 3 0 0 0

Be sure to use proper left hand technique when playing chords for maximum tone and control. Remember to keep your thumb firmly anchored against the back of the neck. Your fingers should be curled inward toward the fretboard and only the tips of your fingers should be touching the strings. Don't grab the neck with your whole hand; no other parts of your fingers or hand should be touching the neck or any of the other strings. Place your fingertips just to the left of (behind) the fret, pressing the strings inward toward the neck. When strumming chords, pivot from your elbow and keep your wrist straight; the strumming motion should come from your elbow. When playing single notes, use more wrist.

One of the hardest things for a beginner to conquer is the ability to play a clean, fully sustained chord without buzzing strings, muted or dead notes. Make sure your left hand is fretting the proper notes and your fingers aren't accidentally touching any of the other strings. Pick each string individually with your right hand, one note at a time. If any of the open strings are deadened or muted, try *slightly* adjusting your fingers. If any of the fretted notes are buzzing, you probably aren't pressing down hard enough with your fingers. It will be difficult at first and might hurt a little, but don't get discouraged. With time and practice, you'll build up callouses on your fingertips. Before you know it, playing chords will be second nature, and your fingers will hardly feel it at all.

Once you have the chords sounding clean and the strumming motion down, the next step is to learn how to change chords quickly and cleanly. Focus on where each finger needs to move for the next chord. Sometimes one or more of your fingers will be able to stay in the same place. Avoid taking your hand completely off the neck. Instead, try to move your whole hand as little as possible and make smaller finger adjustments to change from one chord to the next. When you can change from chord to chord seamlessly, you'll be able to play complete songs.

Open Chord Blues

The following is an example of a *chord progression* and is written on a musical *staff*. A staff is the group of horizontal lines on which music is written. The chord names above the staff show which chord to play, and a *rhythm slash* simply means to strum the chord. In this chord progression, strum each chord twice, using all downstrums. This example also uses *repeat signs* (play through the progression and repeat it again). Listen and play along with the backing track to hear how it should sound. Keep practicing and try to change chords in time without stalling or missing a beat. Count along out loud with each strum, in time and on the beat. Start out slowly if you need to and gradually get it up to speed.

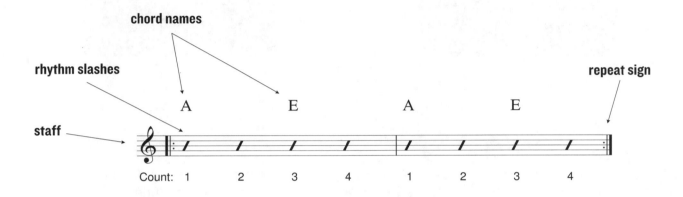

Major Blues

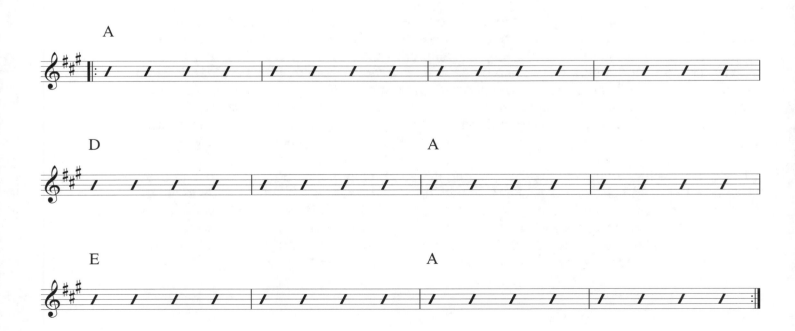

14

Minor Blues

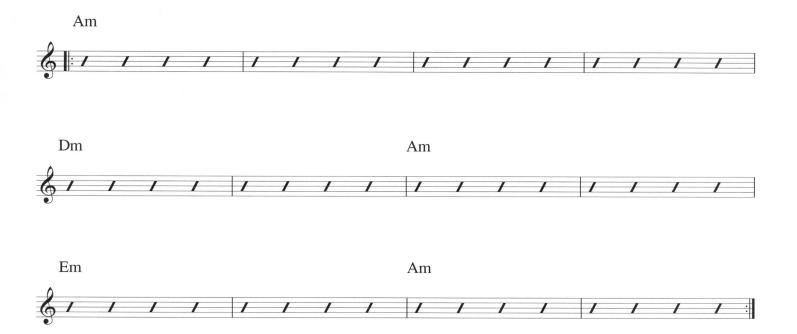

Quick Tip!

MAKE SURE YOUR GUITAR IS SET UP PROPERLY

Beginners don't usually realize that their new guitar may need to be set up for it to play comfortably. A proper set up will ensure that the strings are at the correct height. If they're too high off the neck, it will be harder to press the strings down. You'll also want to check the neck adjustment to be sure your guitar neck has the proper curve. Even right out of the box, new guitars need adjusting. This oversight can cause many beginners to give up in frustration before giving it a fair chance on a properly adjusted instrument.

Rhythm Notation

You don't need to read traditional music notation in order to play guitar, but it's helpful to understand a little bit about the concept of rhythm and timing. In most popular rock and blues, music is divided into *measures* of 4 beats. When a band counts off "One, two, three, four" at the beginning of a song, it represents one complete measure of music. Different types of notes are held for different durations within a measure. For example, a *quarter note* gets one beat because a quarter note is held for one quarter of a measure.

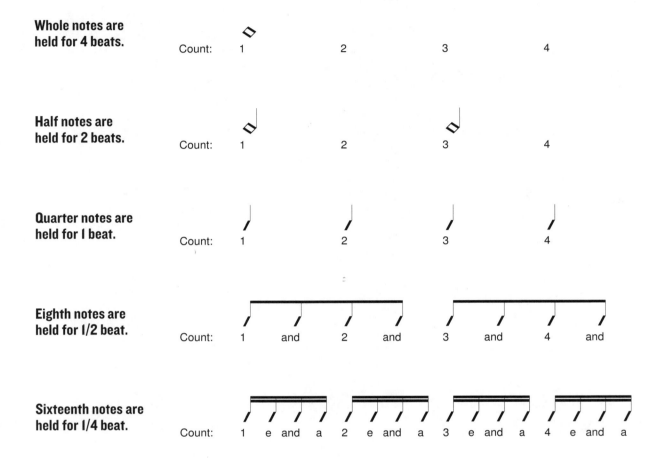

A *tie* is a curved line connecting one note to the next. If two notes are tied, strike only the first one and let it ring out through the duration of the second note (or 'tied' note).

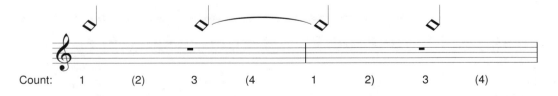

A *dot* after a note increases its value by another 1/2 of its original value. In the following example the half notes are dotted, so they are held for 3 beats.

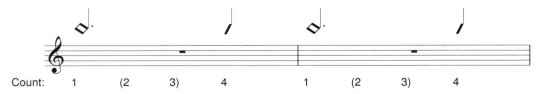

Tablature Explanation

Tablature (or *tab*) is a number system for reading notes on the neck of a guitar. It does not require you to have knowledge of standard music notation. This system was designed specifically for the guitar. Most music for guitar is available in tab. Tablature is a crucial and essential part of your guitar playing career.

The six lines of the tablature staff represent each of the six strings. The top line is the thinnest (highest pitched) string. The bottom line is the thickest (lowest pitched) string. The lines in between are the 2nd through 5th strings. The numbers placed directly on these lines show you the fret number to play the note at. At the bottom, underneath the staff, is a series of numbers. These numbers show you which left hand fingers you should use to fret the notes.

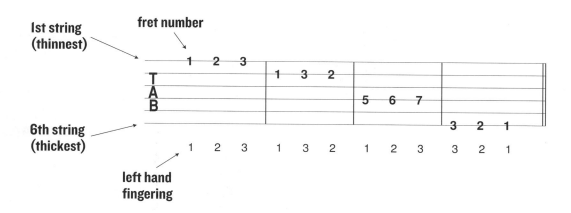

Chords can also be written in tab. If there are several numbers stacked together in a column, those notes should be played or strummed at the same time. Here are the chords you've already learned with the tablature written out underneath each diagram. Since the fingerings are shown on the chord diagrams, we won't bother to repeat them underneath the tab.

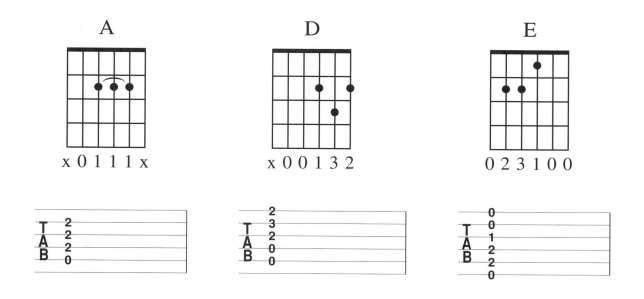

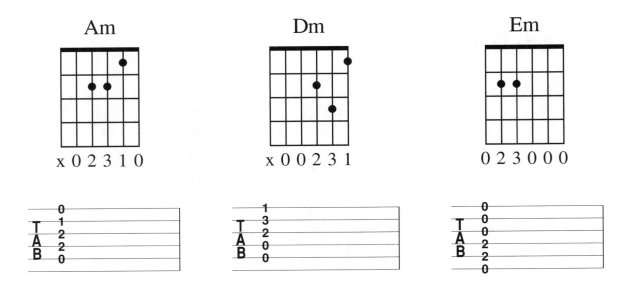

Blues

The following is a basic blues riff in the key of A. This riff is made up of two note chords shown on the tab staff. The chord names above the staff are there as a reference to show you what the basic harmony is while you play along.

This riff should sound very familiar - it's used more than any other blues progression. Plenty of rock and blues classics are played entirely with this one riff repeated over and over. It is made up of 12 measures (or *bars*) of music, called the *12-bar blues*.

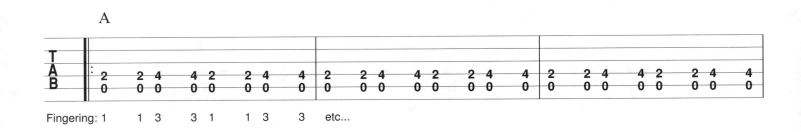

Fingering: 1   1 3   3 1   1 3   3   etc...

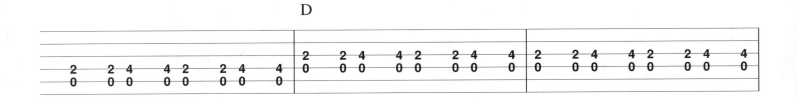

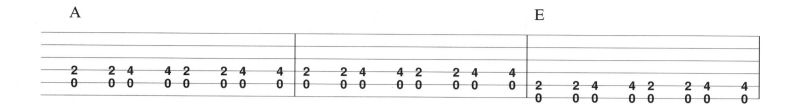

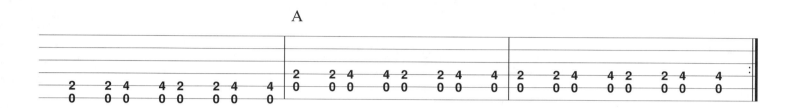

Blues is played with a *shuffle feel*, also called a triplet feel. This example was written in eighth notes, and the second eighth note of each beat should lag a little. This is referred to as triplet feel because the beat is actually divided by thirds, counted as if there were three eighth notes per beat instead of two. The first part of the beat gets 2/3 of a beat, and the second part only gets 1/3.

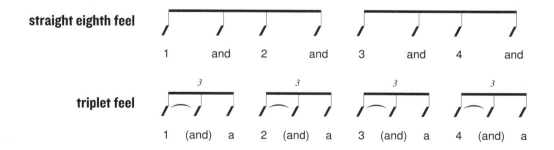

Shuffle feel is a much easier concept to understand by hearing it. Listen to the backing track, count along and try to get the triplet feel in your head. Also, check out almost any blues standard, slow or fast, and you'll probably recognize a shuffle feel being used.

Chapter I Overview

1) The different types of guitars used in blues music are:

   Solid Body Electric - great for distortion sounds and lead guitar.
   Acoustic - good for classic, old school blues, fingerpicking, and
      intimate performances.
   Hollow Body Electric - usually has two F-holes on the front to
      help generate a fuller tone.

2) Minor chords have a sad or melancholy sound; major chords have a
   happy or bright sound.

3) The most commonly used blues chord combination is referred to
   as a I - IV - V progression. To find these chords in any key, build
   chords on the 1st, 4th and 5th degrees (notes) of the scale.

4) When strumming, pivot your arm from the elbow.

5) The tablature staff consists of six horizontal lines representing
   the strings on the guitar. The numbers placed on these lines represent
   the frets you play the notes on.

Recording session at Horizon Music Studio.

John onstage at Toad's Place in New Haven, CT

CHAPTER 2

The Minor Pentatonic Scale

Minor pentatonic scales are the most commonly used scales for playing rock and blues solos. The pentatonic is a five note scale, or an abbreviated version of the full natural minor scale. The word "pentatonic" comes from the greek words, "penta" (five) and "tonic" (the keynote).

Memorize and practice this scale; it's the one you'll use most often for playing melodies and leads. There are five different positions of this scale, each beginning on a different note of the scale. All five positions are shown here in tab. To the right of each tab staff is a scale diagram. These are similar to the chord diagrams we've previously used. A scale diagram shows you all the notes in the scale within a certain position on the neck. The stacked numbers below the diagram indicate the fingering for the notes on each string.

1st Position Am Pentatonic Scale

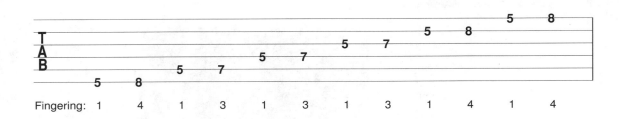

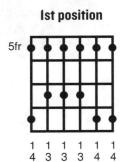

2nd Position Am Pentatonic Scale

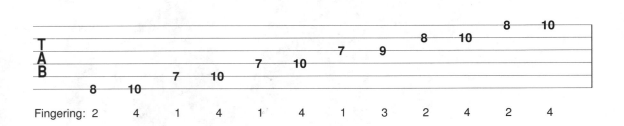

3rd Position Am Pentatonic Scale

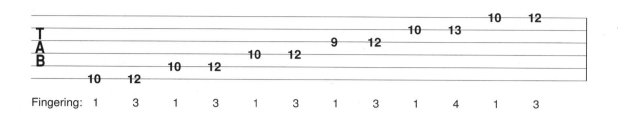
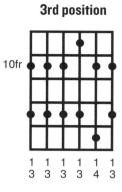

3rd position

Fingering: 1   3   1   3   1   3   1   3   1   4   1   3

4th Position Am Pentatonic Scale

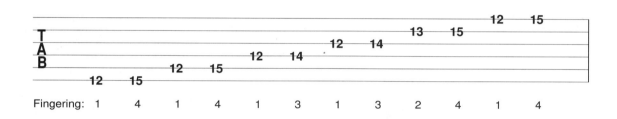
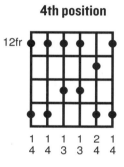

4th position

Fingering: 1   4   1   4   1   3   1   3   2   4   1   4

5th Position Am Pentatonic Scale

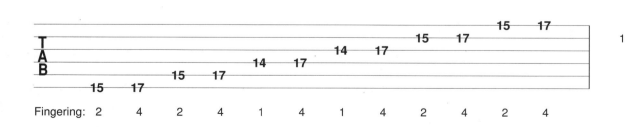
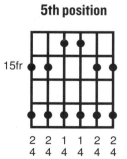

5th position

Fingering: 2   4   2   4   1   4   1   4   2   4   2   4

23

Minor Pentatonic Scale Fretboard Diagram

Once you have all five positions of the minor pentatonic scales mastered, you'll be able to play solos in any position on the neck. Remember that there are only five different name notes in the scale, and the different positions are just groupings of these same notes in different octaves and different places on the neck. The 4th and 5th positions from the previous page can be transposed one octave lower (shown below in the fretboard diagram). Notice how each positon overlaps the next; the left side of one position is the right side of the next one and so on. Think of these scale positions as building blocks (like Legos). When soloing, you can move from position to position and play across the entire fretboard.

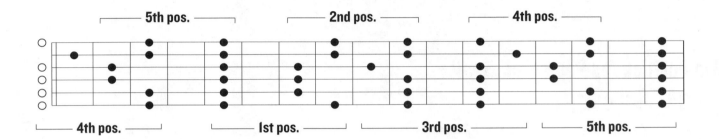

Alternate Picking

Consistent use of alternate picking is a very good habit for you to have. Alternate picking allows you to play solos with much more control and accuracy. Practice playing all of the minor pentatonic scale positions using alternate picking. Play each position ascending and descending at a steady, even tempo until the picking motion feels natural.

The following symbols are used to show picking (or strumming) directions:

⊓ - downpick (pick down toward the floor)

∨ - uppick (pick up toward the ceiling)

Lead Patterns

The following examples are standard lead pattern exercises, designed to help you build coordination and learn how to begin using the minor pentatonics for playing leads. Use alternate picking and the metronome to start out slowly and get the rhythm. Memorize the patterns and gradually speed up the tempo. Before you know it, you'll be playing blazing rock and blues guitar solos.

Double Lead Pattern

Here is the 1st position Am pentatonic scale played using a doubling pattern. Play the notes on the 5th through 2nd strings twice as you travel up and down the scale. Use alternate picking and a steady, even tempo.

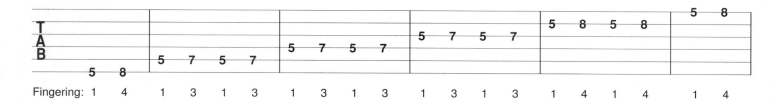

Fingering: 1 4 1 3 1 3 1 3 1 3 1 3 1 3 1 4 1 4 1 4

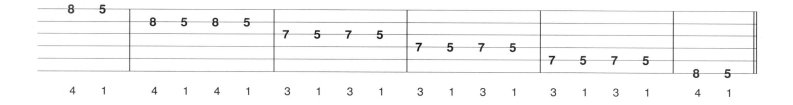

4 1 4 1 4 1 3 1 3 1 3 1 3 1 3 1 3 1 4 1

Now let's take the same double lead pattern and transpose it to the 2nd positon. Once you've got these two memorized, transpose the pattern to the other positions of the pentatonic scale.

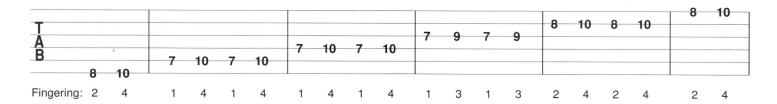

Fingering: 2 4 1 4 1 4 1 4 1 4 1 3 1 3 2 4 2 4 2 4

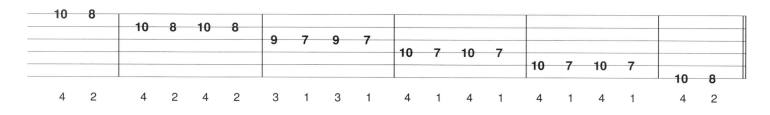

4 2 4 2 4 2 3 1 3 1 4 1 4 1 4 1 4 1 4 2

Triplet Lead Pattern

Here is the 1st position Am pentatonic scale played in groups of three notes, or triplets.
Count "one - two - three, one - two - three" out loud while you play through this exercise
to get the triplet feel in your head.

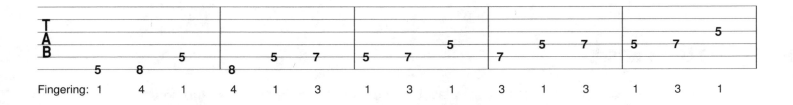

Fingering: 1   4   1   4   1   3   1   3   1   3   1   3   1   3   1

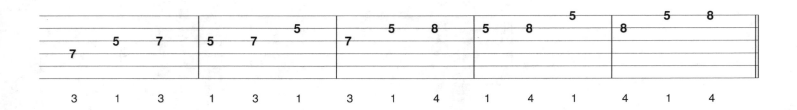

3   1   3   1   3   1   3   1   4   1   4   1   4   1   4

Now let's play the same pattern in reverse, back down the scale in triplets.

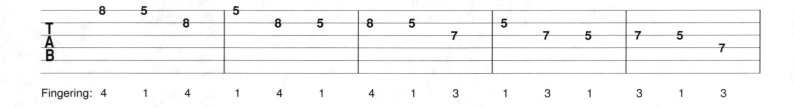

Fingering: 4   1   4   1   4   1   4   1   3   1   3   1   3   1   3

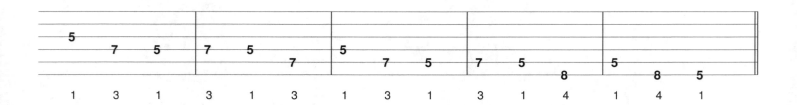

1   3   1   3   1   3   1   3   1   3   1   4   1   4   1

Practice every position of the Am pentatonic scale using the tripet lead pattern and alternate picking. The 2nd position ascending and descending triplet patterns are shown below.

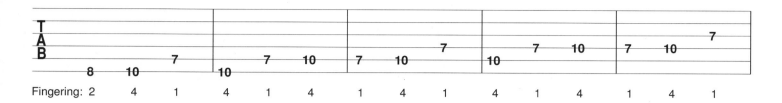

Fingering: 2   4   1   4   1   4   1   4   1   4   1   4   1   4   1

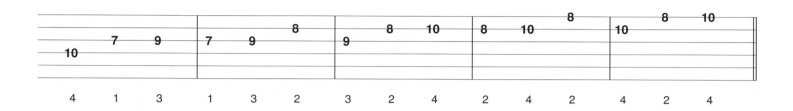

4   1   3   1   3   2   3   2   4   2   4   2   4   2   4

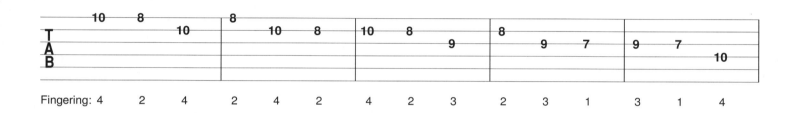

Fingering: 4   2   4   2   4   2   4   2   3   2   3   1   3   1   4

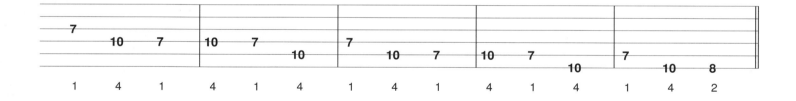

1   4   1   4   1   4   1   4   1   4   1   4   1   4   2

Quick Tip!

PLAY SLOWLY AT FIRST

When learning something new, don't start out trying to play it as fast as possible. Take things slowly at first; play slow enough so you don't keep making mistakes. Build your speed over time. A great tool for learning to build speed gradually is a metronome. This is a device that clicks at an adjustable rate that you set. A metronome allows you to gauge your progress each day. By playing along with the click, you learn to play in time with other instruments.

Lead Techniques

Bending

Now let's learn some lead guitar techniques that will add expression to your playing. Bends are a very soulful way of creating emotion with the guitar, using flesh against steel to alter and control pitches. All guitarists have their own unique, signature way of bending notes.

The row of tab staffs below show bends using the 3rd, 4th or 1st fingers. The "B" above the staff indicates a bend, and the arrow with a "1" above it means to bend the note one whole step in pitch.

First try the 3rd finger bend. While fretting the note with your 3rd finger, keep your first two fingers down on the string behind it and push upward using all three fingers. This will give you added coordination and control. Use the same technique for the 4th finger bend, using all four fingers to bend the string upward. The 1st finger bend will probably be the hardest since you are only using one finger to bend the string. In some situations, you may even pull the string downward with your first finger to bend the note.

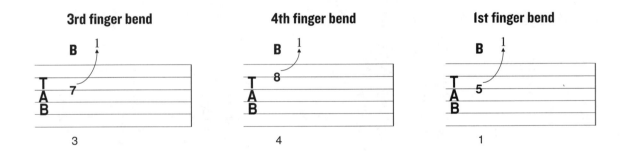

The following example shows what the bends might look like in context when playing a solo in the 1st position A minor pentatonic scale. Play through this exercise and start to get a feel for how to incorporate bends into your own riffs.

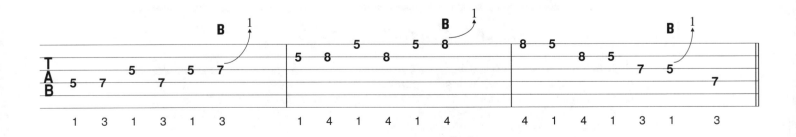

Hammer Ons

A hammer on is also a widely used lead technique. On the staff below, you'll see a slur connecting one tab number to the next. This indicates that only the first tab number is picked; the second note is not struck. The "H" above the slur indicates a hammer on.

To play a hammer on, pick the first note and then push down the next note using just your left hand finger (without picking it). Play through the following series of hammer ons to see how you can use them with the minor pentatonic scale.

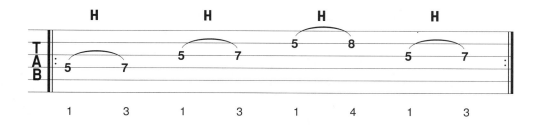

Pull Offs

Pull offs are the opposite of hammer ons. Pick the first note and pull or snap your finger off the string to the get the second note. Your first finger should already be in place, fretting the second note in advance. The "P" above each slur below indicates a pull off.

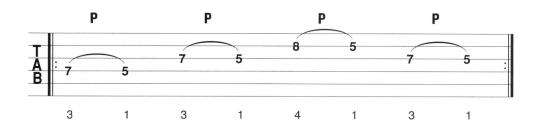

Complete Blues Lead

Here's a solo that uses all of the previous lead techniques in various positions on the neck. In the 11th measure, there's an example of a bend and release: after bending the note, gradually release the bend to the note's original pitch.

Download the backing track from www.rockhousemethod.com and practice playing along with the band. This is a I - IV - V progression in A that also uses a shuffle feel. The chord names above the tab staff are there for a reference to show you where the changes are.

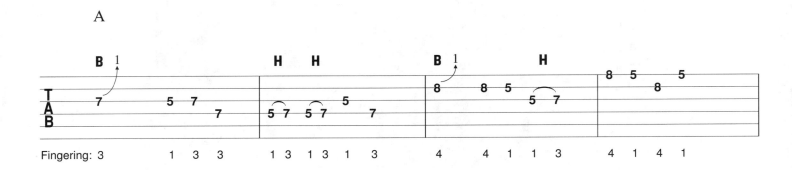

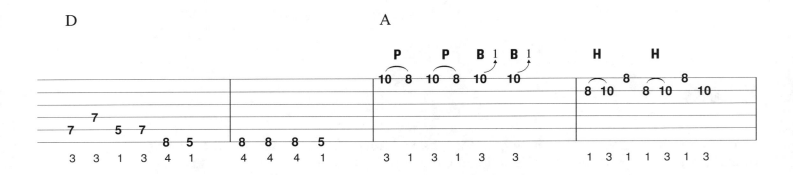

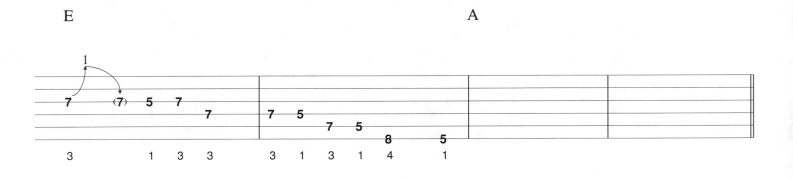

30

Chapter 2 Overview

1) The minor pentatonic scale is a five note scale used widely in rock and blues.

2) There are five different positions of the minor pentatonic scale, each beginning on one of the five notes in the scale.

3) A triplet is a rhythmic pattern that groups three notes for each beat.

4) When bending a note, use all of the left hand fingers before the note you are bending to help push up and control the note.

5) A hammer on is produced by pushing your finger down onto the neck with force; do not pick the note.

6) A pull off is produced by snapping or pulling your finger off from one note to the next without picking the second note.

House of Blues is the Home of Live Entertainment.

Have an intimate yet high energy experience at one of our many venues across the country.

CHAPTER 3

Creating a Great Blues Sound

Effect pedals (or *stomp boxes*) are often used to enhance or distort a guitar's tone. There are many different types of effects. The most popular effects used for blues guitar are overdrive, distortion, chorus, delay, reverb, and wah wah. Below are a few of the most common ones. Take a trip to your local music store and try out a variety of effect pedals to hear which ones sound good to you.

Overdrive Pedal

A distortion or overdrive pedal simulates the sound of the guitar's signal being overdriven, giving it a fuzz tone. Overdrive can be used in different degrees. Light distortion will give the sound a warm, round, or full tone. Using heavy distortion gives the guitar a heavy metal tone.

Chorus Pedal

A chorus pedal creates the sound of a few guitars played at once. A chorus doubles the original signal with a very slight delay, causing a wavy tone that simulates a chorus of guitars.

Wah Wah Pedal

A wah wah pedal is a foot activated pedal that you can "play" with your foot while playing the guitar. The pedal gets rocked back and forth by your foot and gives the guitar a talking, wah wah type sound. What a wah wah pedal actually does is sweep quickly back and forth between extreme bass and extreme treble driven by the movement of your foot.

Amplifier Gain

Turning up the gain knob on an amplifier overdrives the signal and creates distortion. Use small amounts of gain for a warm, thick tone. Using high gain will cause heavy distortion. Use the gain in conjunction with the amplifier's master volume control to set the desired tone and level of the sound.

Blues Riffs That Will Make Yo Mama Scream

Here's a collection of little riffs that will help you start building your own bag of tricks. These riffs use various positons of the Am pentatonic scales, and incorporate all of the techniques we've covered so far. You can play all of these riffs at different speeds, with or without a shuffle feel, starting on any beat you choose. Any one of these is a good choice when soloing and improvising. Try coming up with some of your own variations.

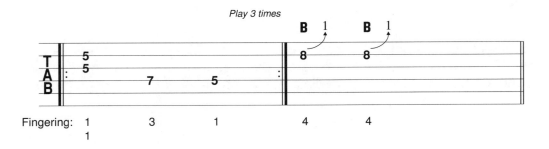

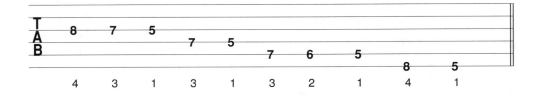

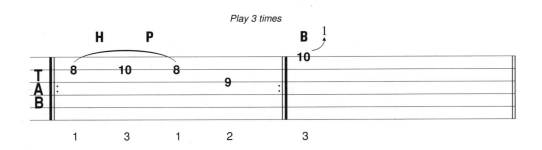

34

Play 4 times

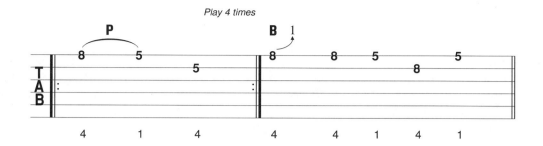

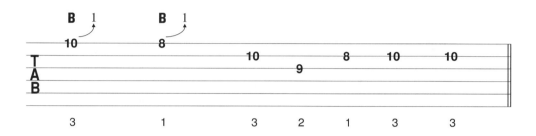

Quick Tip!

DEVELOP GOOD PRACTICE HABITS

Knowing how to practice efficiently will accelerate your progress. Set aside a certain amount of time for practicing and have a routine that reviews all of the techniques you know. Create your own exercises that target weaknesses in your playing. It's important to experiment and get creative as well; try things fast or slow, light or hard, soft or loud.

The B. B. Box

The B.B. box is a section of the minor pentatonic scale that overlaps the 1st and 2nd positions. The name refers to the great B.B. King because he bases a lot of his soloing around this scale. The following fretboard diagram indicates which notes are in the B.B. Box (in the key of Am) using solid black dots. The open circles show the minor pentatonic scale notes in the surrounding positions. Refer to the tab staff below the diagram for the proper fingering.

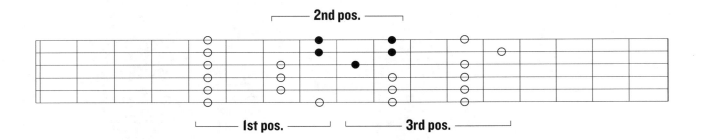

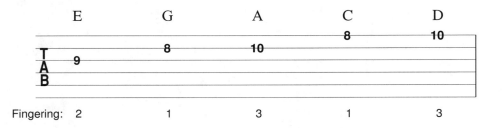

Fingering: 2   1   3   1   3

Above each tab number is its note name. Notice that A (the *root note*) is in between the other notes of the scale. The B.B. Box takes the five notes of the minor pentatonic scale and puts the root note in the middle. This position allows you to play around the root note, playing a few notes up or a few notes down from it. This is also the way many blues singers arrange their vocal melodies. The B.B. Box is great for soloing off the vocal melody or for trading riffs back and forth with the singer.

Shuffle Blues Rhythm

This progression incorporates chords and single notes to make up the rhythm. This standard blues rhythm is in A and uses a I - IV - V progression. Practice along with the backing track to get the timing and the shuffle feel.

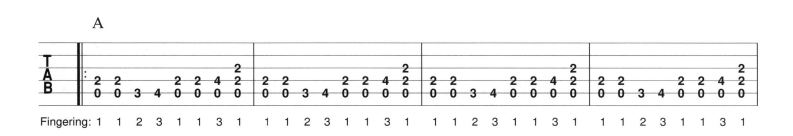

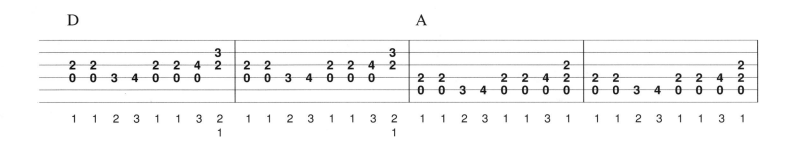

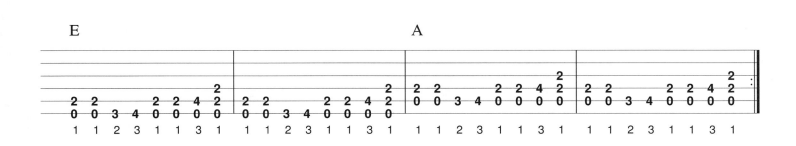

Full Blues Lead

Here's an example of a solo that can be played over the shuffle blues rhythm you've just
learned. This solo incorporates bends, hammer ons and pull offs in a variety of positions.
The riff in the first measure is one of the most commonly used blues riffs; it can be heard
in countless blues guitar solos. After you've got this solo down, try to create your own using
all of the lead techniques and positions of the Am pentatonic scales.

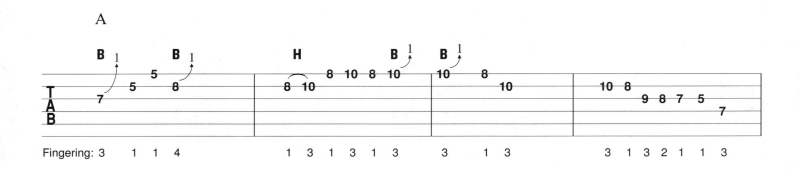

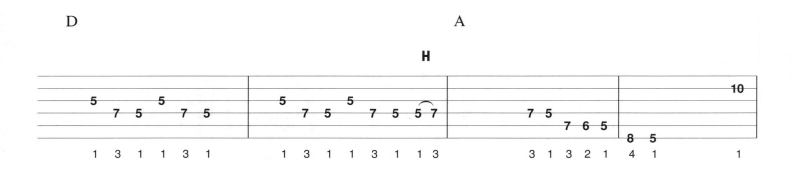

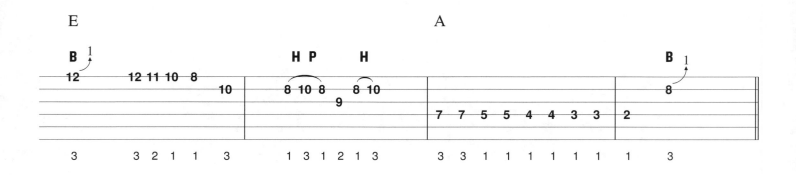

Chapter 3 Overview

1) A riff is a small phrase or group of notes played within a lead or song.

2) Effect pedals (stomp boxes) can be used to enhance your sound. The most popular effects used for blues guitar are: overdrive, distortion, chorus, delay, reverb, and wah wah.

3) The **B.B. Box** is a five note section of the minor pentatonic scale between the 1st and 2nd positions, made popular by guitarist **B.B. King**. These five notes can be used to play entire blues leads; it's like a "hot spot" within the minor pentatonic.

4) Shuffle rhythms are commonly used to create the famous blues feel heard in many blues songs.

CHAPTER 4

Barre Chords

Let's begin this section by expanding your chord vocabulary. The following full barre chords contain no open strings, so they are *moveable* chords; you can transpose them to any fret. After mastering these chords, you'll be able to play in any key and position on the guitar.

6th String Barre Chords

The first chord is F major. This chord is especially difficult to play because you need to barre across all six strings with your 1st finger, then add the other three notes as well. Pick out each note individually to make sure the chord sounds clean.

1 3 4 2 1 1

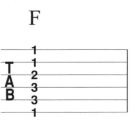

Notice that the lowest note of the chord is F, the *root note*. Using the musical alphabet, you can move barre chords up the neck and change them to any chord in the scale. Use the following chart to find any chord along the 6th string by moving the F chord. The name of the chord will change depending on which fret you move the chord to.

6th string notes (F chord)	E	F	F♯	G	G♯	A	A♯	B	C	C♯	D	D♯	E
fret number	Open	1	2	3	4	5	6	7	8	9	10	11	12

Once you've learned the F barre chord, simply lift your 2nd finger and you'll have the Fm barre chord. The F7 (also called the *F dominant seventh*) barre chord is only slightly different from the F as well; just reposition your 4th finger and you've got it. Dominant seventh chords are often used in blues as substitutes for major chords.

Fm

1 3 4 1 1 1

Fm

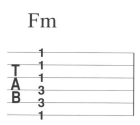

```
T   1
A   1
    1
B   3
    3
    1
```

F7

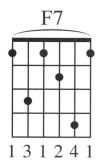

1 3 1 2 4 1

F7

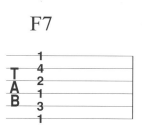

```
T   1
A   4
    2
B   1
    3
    1
```

5th String Barre Chords

The B♭ major barre chord is played at the 1st fret with the root note on the 5th string. This chord has a third finger barre. Make sure the 1st and 6th strings are muted and not strummed. Use the chart below to transpose this chord to any other fret along the 5th string.

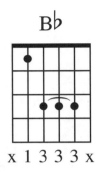

Bb

x 1 3 3 3 x

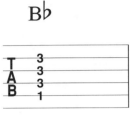

Bb

```
T    3
A    3
     3
B    1
```

5th string notes (B♭ chord)	A	B♭	B	C	C#	D	D#	E	F	F#	G	G#	A
fret number	Open	1	2	3	4	5	6	7	8	9	10	11	12

Quick Tip!

ALWAYS TUNE YOUR GUITAR

Make sure your guitar is in tune every time you play it. You could be playing all of the right notes, but they'll sound incorrect if you haven't tuned up. Even if only one string is slightly out of tune, the simplest of chords will sound bad. It's a good idea to stop and check your tuning from time to time while practicing.

The B♭m and B♭7 barre chords are played using a 1st finger barre. Once you have them mastered, try transposing both chords to other frets using the 5th string chart on the previous page.

B♭m

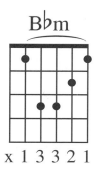

x 1 3 3 2 1

B♭m

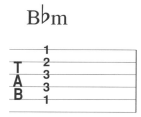

```
    1
T   2
A   3
B   3
    1
```

B♭7

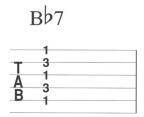

x 1 3 1 4 1

B♭7

```
    1
T   3
A   1
B   3
    1
```

Understanding the 12 Bar Blues Concept

12-bar blues is a progression, based on the I - IV - V chords, that is 12 measures long. Most blues music is made up of 12-bar blues progressions; 12 measures of music that repeat throughout the song. This particular example combines barre chords and single notes, and is in the key of A. The single notes at the end of each measure are played with the 1st and 3rd fingers in the same positon as each chord. Play along with the backing track to get the shuffle feel.

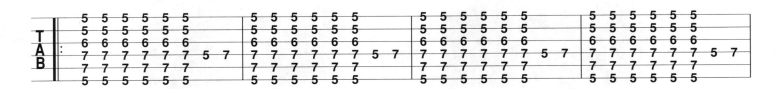

Single Note Blues Rhythm

Here's a shuffle rhythm guitar progression consisting of all single notes. This pattern is a good example of a *riff*. The riff is outlined in the 1st measure, and as the progression follows a 12-bar blues, the riff is transposed to each new chord. This example is also based around a I - IV - V chord change in the key of D (D - G - A). Once you have this progression down, try to create some of your own single note riff rhtyhms.

D

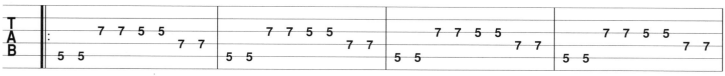

Fingering: 1 1 3 3 1 1 3 3   1 1 3 3 1 1 3 3   1 1 3 3 1 1 3 3   1 1 3 3 1 1 3 3

G   D

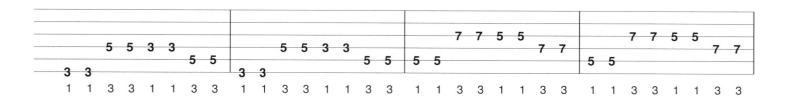

1 1 3 3 1 1 3 3   1 1 3 3 1 1 3 3   1 1 3 3 1 1 3 3   1 1 3 3 1 1 3 3

A   D

1 1 3 3 1 1 3 3   1 1 3 3 1 1 3 3   1 1 3 3 1 1 3 3   1 1 3 3 1 1 3 3

Transposing the Minor Pentatonic Scale

You can solo over the single note blues rhythm by transposing the minor pentatonic scale to D. Each of the five positions can be moved to a different fret, allowing you to solo in any key anywhere on the fretboard. For instance, if you were to move all of the Am pentatonic scale positions two frets (one whole step) higher, you would be playing in B.

The following chart shows the minor pentatonic scale in some popular keys, indicating where each position starts by fret. Choose a key from the left hand column and follow the chart across to see which fret each position starts on. Since an octave is only 12 frets, some positions can be played in two different places on the neck.

key	1st position	2nd position	3rd position	4th position	5th position
A	5th & 17th frets	8th fret	10th fret	12th fret & open	3rd & 15th frets
C	8th fret	11th fret	13th & 1st frets	3rd & 15th frets	6th & 18th frets
E	12th fret & open	3rd & 15th frets	5th & 17th frets	7th fret	10th fret
G	3rd & 15th frets	6th & 18th frets	8th fret	10th fret	13th & 1st frets
B	7th & 19th frets	10th fret	12th fret	14th & 2nd frets	5th & 17th frets
D	10th fret	13th & 1st frets	3rd & 15th frets	5th & 17th frets	8th fret
F	1st & 13th frets	4th & 16th frets	6th & 18th frets	8th fret	11th fret

Chapter 4 Overview

1) Barre chords are moveable chords. They can be transposed and played at any fret along the neck; the root note determines the name of the chord.

2) Dominant seventh chords are commonly used in blues progressions as substitutes for major chords.

3) A 12-bar blues progression is a standard blues progression that is 12 measures in length using the I - IV - V chords.

4) The minor pentatonic scale positions can be transposed to any key. A few popular keys to learn them in are A, D and E.

Come visit us at one of our House of Blues Club venues where you can enjoy southern-inspired cuisine in our restaurant.

Experience an intimate fine dining, entertainment and lounge experience at the House of Blues Foundation Room.

CHAPTER 5

Lead Techniques

Slides

In the following example, slide from note to note without lifting your finger off the fretboard. The "S" above the staff indicates a slide and the line between the notes shows the direction of the slide (up or down the neck). If there is a slur connecting two or more notes, pick only the first note and slide directly to the next without picking. You can perform slides using any finger, but you'll probably use first and third finger slides more often. This exercise is played using the first position Am pentatonic scale. After you get this down, try using the slide technique in other positions as well.

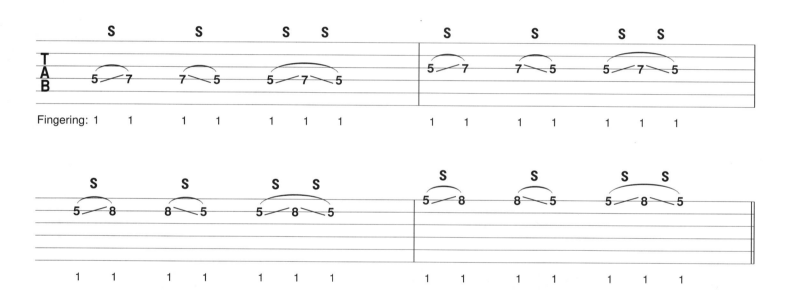

Vibrato

Vibrato is the small, fast shaking of a note. Vibrato is indicated by a squiggly line above the staff, extending out from a note. While sustaining a note, shake your finger slightly and "dig in" to the note to slightly vibrate the pitch and give it more expression. Vibrato can also be applied while bending.

Dead Strums

Here's a rock blues progression that incorporates dead strums, performed by muting the strings with your left hand and strumming the muted strings. These muted notes are shown using x's on the tab staff below. Pay attention to the picking symbols underneath the staff to show you when to upstrum or downstrum. This particular example places dead strums between most of the normal strums, giving the progression more of percussive sound and a rock feel. This example is also played in a shuffle feel. Jam along with the backing track until you have the groove, then try soloing over the progression using the Am pentatonic scale in every position.

Blues Riffs That Will Make Yo Mama Scream Part 2

Now let's add another set of blues riffs to your bag of tricks. These riffs incorporate all of the lead techniques over several positions of the Am pentatonic scale. The last riff uses a double stop slide (sliding two notes at once). After mastering these riffs, try transposing them to other keys and positions on the fretboard.

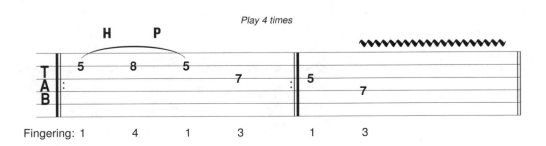

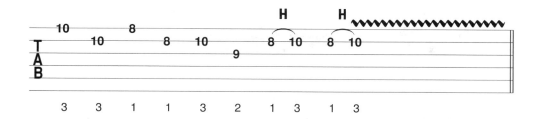

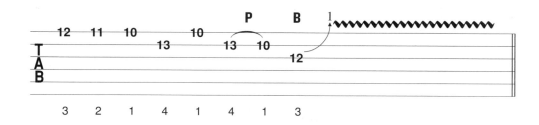

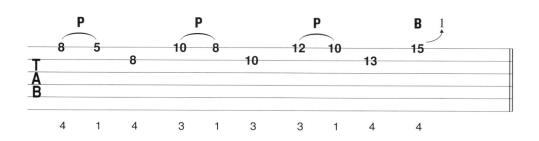

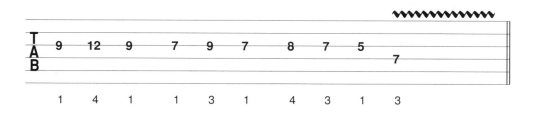

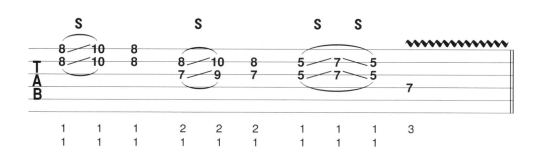

Open Chord Blues Progression in Em

The following progression uses some new open chord variations and suspensions. The chord diagrams show the fingerings for the chords used in this exercise. Notice that the fingering for the Em chord has been varied slightly in order to make it easier to change from chord to chord. Play along with the backing track and get the rhythm down. After you've learned the rhythm part, you can transpose the minor pentatonic scale positions to Em and solo over it. When creating your own solos, use bends, hammer ons, pull offs, slides and vibrato to add personal expression to your playing.

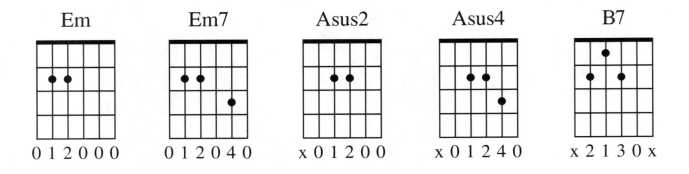

Em   Em7   Asus2   Asus4   B7

0 1 2 0 0 0   0 1 2 0 4 0   x 0 1 2 0 0   x 0 1 2 4 0   x 2 1 3 0 x

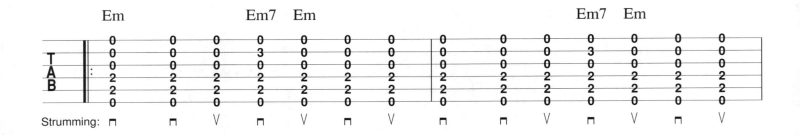

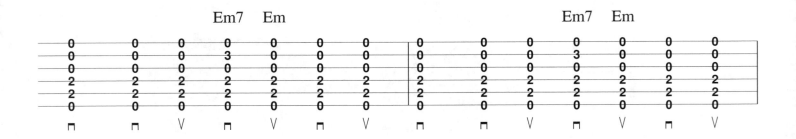

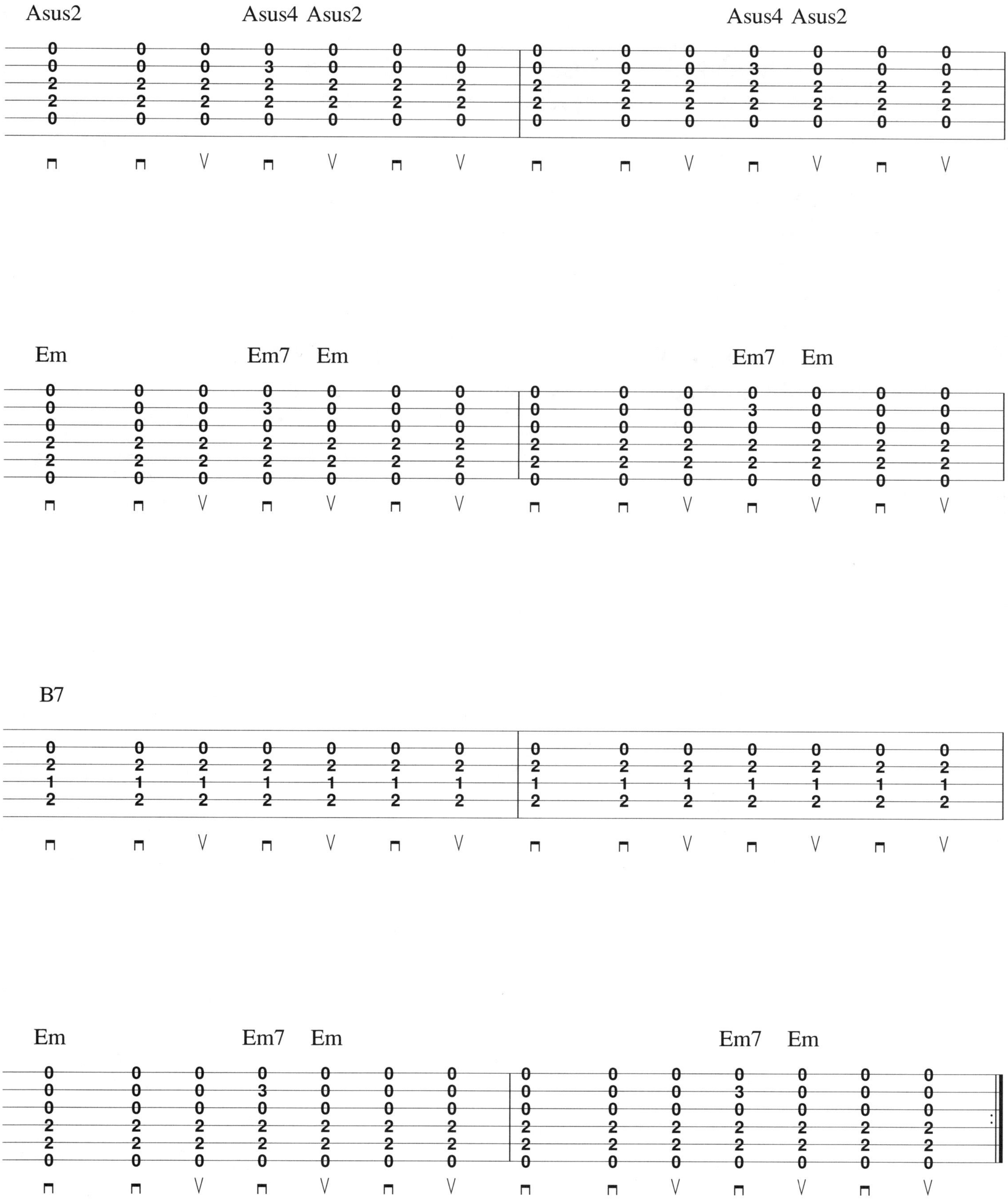
Asus2
Asus4 Asus2
Asus4 Asus2
Em
Em7 Em
Em7 Em
B7
Em
Em7 Em
Em7 Em

Chapter 5 Overview

1) A slide is created by picking a fretted note, then sliding it up or down to another fret while keeping your finger pressed down on the string.

2) Create vibrato by sustaining a note and shaking your finger slightly, vibrating the pitch and giving it more expression.

3) An "x" on a tablature staff indicates a dead or muted note.

4) When creating your own solos, use bends, hammer ons, pull offs, slides and vibrato to add personal expression to your playing.

John rocks The Roseland Ballroom in New York City.

Demonstrating his lighting fast techniques at Music Player Live.

our roots

House of Blues is a home for live music and southern-inspired cuisine in an environment celebrating the African American cultural contributions to blues music and folk art. In 1992, our company converted an historical house in Cambridge, Massachusetts into the original House of Blues®. The original House of Blues opened its doors on Thanksgiving Day, 1992 feeding the homeless before opening to the public. Our commitment to serving the community will always be a priority.

We now have the pleasure of bringing live music to 16 major markets in the U. S. and Canada through our 10 club and 19 arena and amphitheatre venues. Come share the House of Blues experience. Get intimate with your favorite band in our Music Hall or enjoy soulful sounds and eats at our popular weekend Gospel Brunch. Savor down home, southern inspired cooking in the restaurant. Be a VIP for an exclusive night out in the membership club Foundation Room. Celebrate an important event in one of our cool private party rooms and take home a special souvenir from our retail store. We look forward to welcoming you to our house!

our mission

To create a profitable, principled global entertainment company.
To celebrate the diversity and brotherhood of world culture.
To promote racial and spiritual harmony through love, peace, truth,
   righteousness and non-violence.

musical diversity

In our Music Halls, you will find almost every music genre imaginable. Rock n' Roll, Punk, Alternative, Heavy Metal, Rap, Country, Hip-Hop, Rhythm and Blues, Rock en Español, Jazz, Zydeco, Folk, Electronica and many other genres grace our stages. We welcome and celebrate music as a form of art and expression.

Music is a celebration. We design and manage venues with the complete experience in mind. *Best Outdoor Venue. Theatre of the Year. Arena/Auditorium of the Year. Best Large Outdoor Concert Venue. Best Live Music Club of the Year. Talent Buyer of the Year.* From large amphitheatres and arenas to small clubs, our venues and staff garner industry accolades year after year. View our upcoming shows, buy tickets and register for presales and special offers at www.hob.com.

The Gorge Amphitheatre is located in George, WA and has been voted Best Outdoor Arena several years running.

the visual blues

The House of Blues' walls feature American folk art affectionately referred to as the visual blues. With over a thousand original pieces of folk art, House of Blues houses one of the largest publicly displayed folk art collections in America. Like music, these pieces represent a form of artistic expression available to everyone.

philanthropy

Throughout our support of the International House of Blues Foundation (IHOBF), over 50,000 students and teachers experience the Blues SchoolHouse program in our music halls annually. This program explores the history, music and cultural impact of the blues and related folk art through live music, narration and a guided tour of our folk art collection. The program highlights African American cultural contributions and emphasizes the importance of personal expression. The IHOBF is dedicated to promoting cultural understanding and creative expression through music and art (www.ihobf.org).

T
A
B

T
A
B

T
A
B

T
A
B

T
A
B

T
A
B

TAB

TAB

TAB

TAB

TAB

TAB

Level I Blues Guitar
CD Track List

BD = Bass and Drums on the track
BDR = Bass, Drums, and Rhythm Guitar on the track
BDRL = Bass, Drums, Rhythm Guitar and Lead on the track

1 - Introduction
2 - Tuning/Names of the Strings
3 - Parts of the Guitar
4 - Add track 21 from the Electric program Reading Chord Charts here
5 - Major Open Chords A D E
6 - Minor Open Chords Am Dm Em
7 - Open Chord Basic Blues Major Rhythm
8 - Open Chord Basic Blues Minor Rhythm
9 - Open Chord Basic Blues Major and Minor *BDR*
10 - Open Chord Basic Blues Major and Minor *BD*
11 - Basic Blues
12 - Basic Blues *BDR*
13 - Basic Blues *BD*
14 - Minor Pentatonic Scales key of A position 1
15 - Minor Pentatonic Scales key of A position 2
16 - Minor Pentatonic Scales key of A position 3
17 - Minor Pentatonic Scales key of A position 4
18 - Minor Pentatonic Scales key of A position 5
19 - Double Lead Pattern !st Position Scale
20 - Double Lead Pattern 2nd Position Scale
21 - Triplet Lead Pattern 1st Scale Position
22 - Triplet Lead Pattern 2nd Scale Position
23 - Lead Techniques Bending
24 - Lead Techniques Hammer Ons
25 - Lead Techniques Pull Offs
26 - Complete Blues Lead Slow
27 - Complete Blues Lead *BDRL*
28 - Complete Blues Lead *BDR*
29 - Blues Riffs that will make your Momma Scream Riff 1
30 - Blues Riffs that will make your Momma Scream Riff 2
31 - Blues Riffs that will make your Momma Scream Riff 3
32 - Blues Riffs that will make your Momma Scream Riff 4
33 - Blues Riffs that will make your Momma Scream Riff 5
34 - B B Box
35 - Shuffle Blues Rhythm slow
36 - Shuffle Blues Rhythm *BDR*
37 - Shuffle Blues Rhythm *BD*
38 - Full Blues Lead Slow
39 - Full Blues Lead *BDRL*
40 - Full Blues Lead *BDR*
41 - F Major Bar Chord
42 - F Minor Bar Chord
43 - F7th Bar Chord

44 - Bb Major Bar Chord
45 - Bb Minor Bar Chord
46 - Bb7 Bar Chord
47 - Single Note Riff Rhythm Key of D slow
48 - Single Note Riff Rhythm Key of D *BDR*
49 - Single Note Riff Rhythm Key of D *BD*
50 - 12 Bar Blues Progression slow
51 - 12 Bar Blues Progression *BDR*
52 - 12 Bar Blues Progression *BD*
53 - Lead techniques Slides
54 - Lead Techniques Vibrato
55 - Rockin the Blues slow
56 - Rockin the Blues *BDR*
57 - Rockin the Blues *BD*
58 - Blues Riffs that will make your Momma Scream Part Two Riff 1
59 - Blues Riffs that will make your Momma Scream Part Two Riff 2
60 - Blues Riffs that will make your Momma Scream Part Two Riff 3
61 - Blues Riffs that will make your Momma Scream Part Two Riff 4
62 - Blues Riffs that will make your Momma Scream Part Two Riff 5
63 - Blues Riffs that will make your Momma Scream Part Two Riff 6
64 - Open Chord Blues Progression "Key of E"
65 - Open Chord Blues Progression "Key of E" *BDR*
66 - Open Chord Blues Progression "Key of E" *BD*
67 - Conclusion

Music Minus One Backing Tracks

68 – Basic Blues Rhythm *BD* (this track was used with many examples)
69 – Open Chord Blues Progression "Key of E" *BD*
70 – Rockin the Blues *BD*
71 – Single Note Riff Rhythm Key of D *BD*